8
Ke

8
Ke

96-54

Kennedy, Gerald

AUTHOR

I Believe

TITLE

I BELIEVE

I BELIEVE

Gerald Kennedy

ABINGDON PRESS
New York • Nashville

I BELIEVE

Copyright © MCMLVIII by Abingdon Press

Library of Congress Catalog Card Number: 58-5400

Bible quotations, unless otherwise designated, are
from the American Standard Version of the Revised
Bible, copyright, 1929, by the International Council
of Religious Education.

D

SET UP, PRINTED, AND BOUND BY THE
PARTHENON PRESS, AT NASHVILLE,
TENNESSEE, UNITED STATES OF AMERICA

THIS IS FOR MY FATHER

Who went on before

————•◆•————

CONTENTS

I BELIEVE IN GOD

I NEVER MET AN ATHEIST. I HAVE MET A FEW PEOPLE WHO claimed they were atheists. But when we talked it over, it always seemed to me they were objecting to someone else's idea of God rather than insisting that there was no God. There is a story about a man at a convention of atheists who became annoyed because he thought the other delegates were backing down from their atheism. He made a speech against this compromising attitude and ended by saying, "I am a real atheist, thank God!"

We cannot live without God

There are people who will insist they are atheists. For them the words of Tolstoy are to the point. He said that God is he without whom we cannot live. If some people insist there is no God and yet go on living, how shall we explain it? Let us say they go on living because they act as if they had not said it. Tolstoy was right. If a man really did not believe in God, he could not go on living as a man. We have to live as if we believe there is something in this universe that gives our life meaning. And when we face this basic fact in living as men, God has found us.

I do not see how anyone in a day like ours can doubt

that God is real. We have been trying to get along without him for some time, and look at the sorry shape our world is in. We have felt that we ourselves could solve all our problems. We have set ourselves up high and worshiped gods made by our own hands—gods named Science, Progress, Money, Power, Prosperity, Pleasure, Reason, Education, Success. For a while these gods seemed to take the place of the God of our fathers well enough. But they have proved to be false gods. Worshiping them is superstition and not religion. Sometimes they turn their worshipers into monsters, madmen, or dull robots. If we follow them farther, we plunge into the abyss. God is he without whom men cannot live.

The point is that God is not a matter of choice; he is a matter of necessity. We cannot do as we please, cannot take him or leave him. When we go our own way, we go wrong. When we try to build a life or a society without coming to terms with him, we build on the sand. A civilization is always built on a religion. Once men begin to doubt their faith in God, they are on the way down. Experience shows that God is the reality on which life is built. Let a man doubt that he himself is real if he must, but never let him doubt that God is real.

It takes less effort to believe the most difficult doctrines of Christianity than it does to believe the universe began by chance. Men who accept that idea show more willingness to believe the unlikely than the most conservative of Christians. To put blind force in place of God calls for more blind credulity than a thinking man can muster. We turn from such nonsense to the opening words of

10

Genesis, "In the beginning God . . ." The simple words shine in their own light and speak with conviction.

How shall we describe God?

I cannot undertake a profound, philosophical, exhaustive discussion of the nature of God. I am simply writing as a witness, telling what I believe about God. To the lazy, indifferent Christian people of our time I would like to say: "Why don't you take the time to find out what Christianity says about God? You would be ashamed to know as little about how your car operates as you know about what the great Christian thinkers have said about God." Christian people should not be content to take their ideas about God from experts in other fields—who mean well but do not know what the Church has been teaching.

Surely God has left enough signs of his presence to show plain men some things about his nature. For one thing, God is an artist who has given us beauty on every side. Painters, poets, and musicians know we can live in a world that is beyond the world our minds can grasp. It is the world of beauty. Sometimes we need help to see and hear, but you and I have enough appreciation in us to respond to the wonder of God's presence in Nature.

We remember autumn woods, mountains at sunrise, sunsets by the sea, forest groves at noontime, valleys by moonlight. Every place and every season has its special beauty for us. We cannot be a part of it without feeling our hearts rise up in worship. Admiral Byrd in his book *Alone* described his feelings as he watched a day die at the South Pole. He wrote: "The conviction came that that rhythm was too orderly, too harmonious, too perfect to be a product of blind chance—that, therefore, there must be purpose in the whole and that man was part of that whole and not an accidental offshoot."

God is mind

We cannot look at the wonders of the natural world without seeing a great Mind at work. Whether we think of the miracle of the atom or try vainly to understand what billions of light years mean, we cannot escape this conviction: the world reveals a Mind that makes our own minds count for something only as they can recognize this greater Mind. We do not create; we only discover. Most of our thinking is seeing and appreciating the marvels that prove a vast Intelligence at work. The glory of science is that it can reveal this truth. The weakness of science is its pride that assumes these marvels of nature are no longer God's because men have understood them. Nature's laws were not set up by men. They were operating a long time before man appeared.

The greatest scientists recognize how little their minds are beside the Mind revealed in the world of nature. They speak of "thinking the thoughts of God after him." They speak of standing on the ocean shore with a few shells in their hands while the great mystery of God stretches out before them. They speak of the universe as being not a great machine but a great thought. Men are growing dissatisfied with the nineteenth-century theory that nature is a substitute for God. They are driven at last to confess that nature is clear proof of a mighty Mind at work. In the words of Shakespeare, man increasingly

> Finds tongues in trees, books in the runnings brooks,
> Sermons in stones.

God is righteousness

Beside the laws of nature there is the moral law. This would seem to say that God is the champion of the right. He has established an order that holds up good and tears down evil. Any man who is not an idiot knows that the sense of right and wrong is real.

The court of last appeal is the sense of "I ought." Against this we cannot argue, nor can we explain it apart from God. Some people have tried to make conscience out as merely social custom, but for his conscience' sake many a man defies social custom and goes against public opinion. Some people would say conscience is only a matter of education and home training. But every man recognizes the demands of conscience and sees them much alike no matter what his home training or cultural background has been. Every man has a conscience, and every man's conscience tells him he should do what is right and not do what is wrong.

Where does conscience come from? It comes from the God who created the world and men. We have a sense of owing something to the one who made us. Even when no man knows of our fault and there is no chance that any man will ever find it out, still we are guilty in our own eyes. We are guilty because we know there is Another

13

who also knows all about it. How often a sensitive man who shrinks from an unpleasant duty says to himself: "If only God would leave me alone! If only he would let me be comfortable!" But God will not let us alone. When it comes to putting his demands upon us, God neither slumbers nor sleeps.

The moral law shows in the history of nations and societies. The children of Israel discovered it early. In Deborah's song of joy over the fall of an oppressor she says:

> From heaven fought the stars,
> from their courses they fought against Sisera.
> —Judg. 5:20

She knew that the universe itself is against wrong. Israel's prophets saw this so clearly that God became real to them in every event of history. He was the deciding force in battles, in social life, in politics. We can be sure of one thing: no nation founded on injustice can long endure. When men or nations do wrong, they will be punished. In the words of the Old Testament:

> Righteousness exalteth a nation;
> But sin is a reproach to any people.
> —Prov. 14:34

None of this makes sense if we have a blind machine for a world. It makes sense only when we see that back of all our affairs there is God, who protects the good and destroys the evil.

14

God is a person

The Christian truth that takes first place and includes all I have been saying is this: God is a person. This troubles a good many people. They suppose Christians are childish folks who think of God as if he were only a man. Such people prefer to talk about God as a "principle," or an "idea."

Let me make clear what I am *not* saying. I am not making God an old man with a long white beard. The Gospel of John saves us from that mistake by insisting that "God is a Spirit."

But I am saying God is a person. By this I mean he has will, mind, purpose, freedom, self-consciousness. The highest creation we know in the world is a person. The climax of the whole process of creation is a personality. Persons tower over nature and the animal kingdom. We must say God is at least a person, or we would be making him something of less value than a man. Principles and ideas do not mean as much as persons. God may be more than personal; but since we do not know anything that is more, we shall go as high as we know.

God faces men

All of this becomes clear in the Christian experience of being found by God. When God finds a man, that man meets a Divine Person who faces him with personal claims. The man has to do much more than heed a moral principle or adjust his life to the law of right and wrong. He has to go through a personal experience. It is like David's experience when Nathan pointed to him and said, "Thou art the man." It is like Jesus' experience when he heard a voice from out the heavens say, "Thou art my beloved Son."

Until a man finds God and is found by God, he begins at no beginning and he works to no end. In other words, God is not one of the elective courses in the school of life; he is the one required course. Without this course we cannot pass our final examinations. There is nothing to take the place of God. Everything goes wrong without him. Nothing fits into place until a man has put God at the center of his thought and action.

Life has no purpose without God, and no generation should understand that better than ours. For we have most of the things we thought we wanted. We can travel swiftly; we can send messages over vast distances; we can produce more comforts of life than our fathers could imagine. Today the poor can enjoy things which would have been luxuries to the ancient kings. Yet something has gone wrong. We are no longer thrilled to think we will soon produce still more goods, more comforts. All our trinkets have not brought us peace of mind. In spite of our heroic conquests over nature, the feeling haunts us that we spend our time on toys and trivialities, and we are moved by no mighty purposes.

Only God can keep our sense of values straight. William Temple, late Archbishop of Canterbury, once said that the world is like a shop window where some prankster has gone in and changed all the price tags. On the expensive articles he has put the low prices, and on the cheap articles he has put the high prices. We pay more than we should for what does not satisfy us, and we neglect the things we really need. Isaiah's question is for us: "Wherefore do ye spend money for that which is not bread? and your labor for that which satisfieth not?" (Isa. 55:2). People who forget God also forget what is worth striving for.

Without God we cannot have human brotherhood, which is the recognition of each man's worth. If you can rob men of their belief that they are the sons of God, you pave the way for tyranny. This is not just somebody's opinion. This is history. We have only one bulwark against the cheapening of human life. It is to maintain at all costs the Christian belief that God created each man and made him a son of God. Like coins, men have value, not in themselves, but because they bear the stamp of the King.

We can find freedom only in God. God's demands often seem severe, yet they free us more than anything we know. When we try to get away from his demands, we end up as slaves to ourselves or to other men. But when we decide we must obey God rather than men, we feel we have been set free. It is like escaping from a prison. In God's service we find perfect freedom.

All the things that make us men have their roots in God. He is like the air we breathe and the water we drink. Eddie Rickenbacker, the famous flyer, drifted around on a life raft for twenty-one days, hopelessly lost in the Pacific. A friend later asked him what lesson he had learned. "The biggest lesson I learned from that experience," he said, "was that if you have all the fresh water you want to drink and all the food you want to eat, you ought never to complain about anything." So it is with the man who has lost

17

God. He comes to know that God is man's one necessary possession.

I believe in God because he has faced me and laid his claims upon me. Just as a man knows it when he falls in love, or knows it when he thrills to the beauty of nature, so he knows it when God places his demand upon him. Maybe he cannot be as precise as John Wesley and say that it happened about a quarter of nine. But he knows that once he was lost and now he is found, and all his life is changed. The experience makes him humble. He may have learned enough about God to live by, but he now finds the ruling passion of his life is to learn *more* about him.

That is the hope of every Christian. It is the worthiest goal for any man's life. When we have gone far enough to be able to say, "I believe in God," we stand at the beginning of life's great adventure.

CHAPTER TWO

I BELIEVE IN JESUS CHRIST

DO YOU UNDERSTAND EINSTEIN? DO YOU AGREE WITH HIM?"
someone asked Bertrand Russell.

"My answer is no to the first question and yes to the
second," replied the philosopher.

I feel the same way as I try to say what I believe about
Jesus. I shall not try to explain everything about the person of Christ. I am not so sure of myself in this field as
some of my brethren seem to be. When I look at Jesus
Christ, I have to admit there is much in him that is beyond
me. My sense of his mystery and greatness grows on me
with the passing years. I don't mean that Jesus is vague to
me. He is as real as anything I know. But I cannot draw
rigid lines around what Christ is. If I find it hard to say
what my wife means to me, I cannot see how it would be
easy to tell what Jesus Christ means to me. If I must grope
for words to tell how I love my friend, how could anyone
expect me to explain exactly how I love my Lord and how
he loves me?

God was in Christ

I can say one thing with deep conviction and assurance:
I believe that God revealed himself to me and to all men
in Christ. Paul's word seems to me the best: "For in Christ

God reconciled the world to himself instead of counting men's trespasses against them; and he has entrusted me with the message of his reconciliation" (II Cor. 5:19 Moffatt). This is the heart of the Christian's faith in Jesus.

Jesus Christ is what we should expect if God is a person. Being what he is, God must want to reveal himself to his children as completely as they are able to accept him. Nature shows us God, and we cannot turn any place in the world without seeing traces of his presence. But the God who seeks you and me, who cares about *persons,* cannot be revealed in a rock or an ocean. He can be revealed only in a *person.* And that is exactly what the disciples and early Christians declared God did in his Son. They did not all say it the same way, but they all testified that when they saw Jesus, they saw God. The great triumphal shout of the gospel became: God is like Christ.

This idea was not very different from what the Jews believed about God. If we take the Hebrew literally, we read in the book of Judges, "But the spirit of Jehovah clothed itself with Gideon" (6:34). It is men who give God's Spirit legs to walk with, arms to strike with, and a voice to proclaim his will. But what other men have done in part, Jesus Christ did in full.

I do not believe Jesus was different from other men simply because he was supremely good. There is something in Christ that makes it absurd to call him just "a good man." I have known many good men, and a few saints. But none of them could do for me what Jesus Christ does for me, or what he does for any sinner. That is where the mystery comes in, and that is where our minds falter.

20

He is God and he is Man; he is human and he is divine; he is my example and he is my Saviour. And so I go back to the word of Paul. It is simple, but it takes in everything: "God was in Christ reconciling the world unto himself."

Jesus reveals God to man

Some people think of Jesus as a very nice person, who said some beautiful things. We are tempted to think of him as an idealist, or as a poet. But to think of Jesus in this way is to pay him our worst insult. It is to look at him in the way he hated most. He cared nothing for flattery, and he despised the dabblers in religion, who did not take him seriously.

I believe that Jesus Christ is a revelation of God. He is a revelation of the way things really are. He did not say the things we read in the Gospels because they were "nice." He said them because they were true. The Sermon on the Mount does not soar about in the clouds. It walks the solid earth; it states the truth about God's world and about man's life. Students of religion sometimes write volumes and leave out this essential clue to what is real. No book about God is complete until it says not once but many times: "God is like Christ." No Christian truly understands his Lord until he sees him as a practical guide to things as they are.

One day Voltaire lifted his hat when a Catholic procession went by. A friend, who knew how much he opposed the Roman Catholic Church, said in surprise, "Why do you lift your hat?"

Voltaire answered, "It is this way with me and God; I lift my hat but I never speak."

It is that way with a great number of people who do not know Christ. But Christians have learned to speak to God and to hear him speak to them through his Son. And we learn from Jesus that God wants us to come to him even more than we are willing to go.

Jesus teaches us to call God "our Father." From this we learn that we can go to God without fear and even without being worthy. He shows us that God is willing to forgive. How could we be so certain of God's love, which is wider than the sea, if Christ had not showed it to us? As John expressed it, "For God so loved the world, that he gave his only begotten Son, that whosoever believeth on him should not perish, but have eternal life" (3:16). I believe that Jesus reveals God to men.

Jesus shows God's forgiveness

Martin Luther thought deeply about sin and the problem of forgiveness. He once quoted Horace's old rule of the drama: Do not bring a god into the play unless the plot is so hopelessly tangled up that only a god can unravel it. This is exactly what happens to the human plot. Sin is such a tangle that man cannot deal with it. Only God can straighten it out. Jesus brings us a vision of God's love for the sinner. He shows us also the terrible cost of forgiveness. Someone may say that God could simply forgive men and let it go at that. Then we must answer that until men have some sense of what forgiveness means, forgiveness cannot save them.

Let me put this another way. A man may have been bad in his own life; he may hold no high standards of how to act. Then he may forgive another man simply because the man's sin is no worse than what he himself has been doing all along. The man who is forgiven in this way will think the forgiveness has little value—and he will be right. But here is another person who has lived a pure life and hates an evil act with all his heart. Let this man forgive the sinner, and the guilty one falls to his knees in an agony of repentance. It is then a terrible thing to be forgiven. But it is a saving thing.

The Crucifixion shows us something of this mystery. The cross of Christ reveals the price a holy God paid to redeem us. Calvary points to how far God will go to make us free. Out of the death of God's Son comes the power to change evil men into sons of God. I do not understand all that the death of Jesus Christ means. But I know that out of this worst has come the best. In some marvelous way the cross of Christ saves the world through God's action in Jesus.

Jesus is the Saviour of man

We sometimes fail to understand how Jesus Christ is the Saviour of men. Some people think it means that all a man has to do is to say, "I believe in Jesus." Then no matter how big a rascal he is, he will be saved. Too many pious people who claim they have been "saved" are the hardest people to get along with, the meanest people in town. Decent men object to this kind of religion, and they are right. Salvation that does not affect a man's daily actions has no value for God or man.

Charles Wesley said, "O let me commend my Saviour to you." He meant he knew one who could change life and save men from sin. He meant that when Christ finds a man, the man aims higher; he feels compassion; a golden "extra" is added to his life. Jesus saves men from meanness and self-pity and despair. He makes them at peace with themselves and kind to other people. He fills their hearts with a joy unspeakable.

Katharine Hathaway was a lifelong cripple who with God's help built a rich and full life. In *The Little Locksmith,* the story of her life, Miss Hathaway tells of a college friend who always drew out the best in people. This friend's talent was to see in a timid person "something rare and important and to make other people see it too—above all, to make the person in question feel it and be it." She would hold this person, who had been so colorless, up in a certain light, "like a collector showing a rare piece, and the person, in her hands, would suddenly receive a value and importance which made the people who watched the transformation wonder how they could have been so blind as never to have seen it before."

So Jesus draws out the best in people. He did it with those plain men he called to be his disciples. He does it with many people today. How often I ask myself: "What would my life be without Christ?" But for his grace and his love who can tell what meaningless depths I might inhabit? Because of what he has done for me, I want, like Charles Wesley, to commend my Saviour to every man.

24

Jesus is the standard

There is an authority in Jesus that was clear to all who knew him and has been clear to men in every age. He has the final authority that does not depend on force but on its own moral might. Men can never escape Jesus, and they can never capture him. Like their own conscience, Christ stands over against every human effort and every social action. No man or people can ever know peace or security until they have come to terms with Jesus Christ.

The Cross is not a judgment on Jesus, but on the world. That judgment falls on the well-meaning people who did nothing to prevent the Crucifixion, and who tried desperately to escape from one who saw their evil and would not keep quiet about it. They were not afraid of him because of their private sins. But they could not bear to have things changed—could not stand to give up their special privileges. Their ambition, their pride, their lust for comfort, their indifference to the suffering caused by their success—all of this crucified Jesus.

When R. F. Horton was at Oxford, he attended the lectures of T. H. Green. After he came to know the great teacher, young Horton told him about his own vivid and real faith in Christ. Green's brief, intense comment was: "You are very fortunate."

Yes, any man who has a faith in Christ is fortunate. But he is not always comfortable. Faith in Christ is wrought out of life at its worst as well as life at its best. It does not bring us ease or contentment. It puts our life

25

forever under the searching light of one who was perfect. It opens our heart to the terrible, gentle love of one who never lets us go. It means we shall never know one hour of satisfaction with our success if we buy it with our moral failure.

But when we have faith in Christ, we shall never again walk alone. When we bring our life under Christ's control, we go ahead—and what is more, we go ahead on the right road. Every year we walk with him makes his companionship dearer. I believe that God was in Jesus Christ.

CHAPTER THREE

I BELIEVE IN MYSELF

TODAY IT IS QUITE THE THING FOR PEOPLE TO THINK THAT alone and without any help they can do all things. "Any man can do anything he wants to do," say the go-getters and the self-made men. Their voices are shrill, and their words are full of sound and fury. But they mean nothing. These people are pitiful as they try to make life a mere matter of doing something rather than *being* something. The Christian must believe in himself for what he is through the grace of God—and for what he can become.

I must see myself as I am

Men who study how our minds work show us how easy it is to make false pictures of ourselves. In one sense our hardest task is to be honest with ourselves. A recent survey showed that eight out of ten Americans think we could solve all our major problems if we would live by the law of love. But—and note this!—the same survey showed that the same number of Americans—eight out of ten—think *they are* living by the law of love. The trouble is all with other people! The more we understand our own hearts, the more we see that Christianity is right: pride is the root sin. We see ourselves as much finer than we really are.

The world is full of men trying to profit out of other

27

men's work. They are afraid to stand on their own feet, so they wrap and twist themselves around some stronger person. Life is too harsh for them to face, so they cling to some friend or loved one. They stifle and smother that person, and grow weaker and weaker themselves.

Other men who have no safe anchor for their spirits try to rule the lives of others. They growl and they roar. But the cruelest, most demanding men often prove to be frightened half to death when you come to know them. Feeling hopeless and reckless, they build up a picture of a tyrant and try to act the part. But all they do is put on a tyrant's mask. Men long to have people think they are strong and can stand alone, until this longing becomes a lust. People in every walk of life feel this lust, and the clergy are not free of it. Each man thinks he must pass the blows from above on to the men below him.

Most of us would like to be a star. Some of us begin to think we are better than other people. We want the world to know how good we are and to give us the praise we deserve. When we want it enough, we will do anything to win that praise. Public opinion becomes our god, and we are its victims. Plain, everyday honesty could give our lives dignity and meaning, but our desire to please everyone destroys our integrity. We become shadow persons; we are no substance and we are not real. Some men live their whole lives through and do not find their true selves.

Christ helps me understand myself. He helps each one of us become a real person. He gives us the understanding and the power to live noble, heroic, joyous lives. G. K.

Chesterton, who was interested in art and literature and religion, said: "I am quite capable of talking or writing about Dutch gardens or the game of chess; but if I did, I have no doubt that what I would say or write about them would be colored by my view of the cosmos." Only when my view of myself is colored by Jesus Christ will I see myself as I am in the sight of God.

I am a sinner

Too many of us hold the false idea that sin is something modern man has outgrown. We think that men no longer need to be saved—therefore the gospel must be out of date. Too many of us think that if we have enough trinkets to amuse us and enough comfort to surround us, we can be quite happy without bothering about our souls. We have learned much about what men need for their bodies, but we have tried to shut our eyes to the sickness of men's spirits.

Many modern thinkers have studied how people act and why they act as they do. They have told us that men are not evil but only ignorant. This idea has led us into the jungle. We threw our energy into teaching men facts. Then we found out that the man who knows many facts may be more of a threat to society than he was before we "educated" him. It depends on how he uses what he knows.

Not that Christianity is against education—far from it. Christianity is the mother of education. But until we do something to cleanse the heart, a well-trained mind will not automatically lead a man into the kingdom of God.

29

I am a sinner, and I do not know how deep my sin and ignorance are until I begin to look at myself through the eyes of Christ. We never like to face our moral failures and our secret sins. Once we crack the shell of our pride, we look at ourselves with despair. "If this is the truth about me," we say, "what can I expect at the hand of a just God?" Yet no man can be any good until he knows how bad he is—or might be. Before I can really believe in myself, I have to strip myself of my false pride. I have to see myself as a wretched creature, doing the things I know are wrong, a slave to the power of sin. If I try to cover this up, I simply move toward disaster.

The greatest problem for any man is himself. No matter how much I want to be good, no matter how much I promise myself to do better, I always come up against a horrible weakness in my soul. Faith in myself has to begin with this Christian word to every man: "You are a sinner."

I cannot stand alone

Even if God gives us the grace to see ourselves as sinners, we may seek the wrong way out. We may think we can get rid of this evil by ourselves, and save our own lives. We may throw out our chests and shout, "I am the captain of my soul!" God is good enough for the weakling, we seem to say, but I can stand on my own two feet. I have no need of him.

For a time this may work fairly well. I get along happily with my family and my friends and my boss. I have enough money to buy what I need, and I really believe all is well and I can run my life by myself. But soon or late this make-believe world fades. Maybe things just go stale, or I lose my job or my wife. I feel like a lost soul, and I can find no anchor to hold me steady. I try to go on as before, but my very spirit is sick. The world is full of men with such sickness of spirit.

When we live only on the human level and see only this world, soon or late our lives become drab and weak. Certainly one purpose of trouble and suffering is to make us see how empty our lives are without God. As Augustine says, God always wants to give us something, but he cannot when our hands are full, for there is nowhere for him to put it. Driven by our need, we come at last to ask God to do for us what we cannot do for ourselves. It is then that we learn we have been running away from what we really wanted. When at last we confess that we are not strong enough and not good enough to be what we ought to be, then God has his chance to mend our broken lives. But until we have been found by him, we are incomplete. We try to cover up our weakness and to silence our fear, but without God we cannot face life. We cannot stand alone.

I am responsible for what I do

If we could escape the feeling that we are responsible for what we do, and that we ought to be good, we might find peace. Many people try to find peace this way. They blame the lack of good leaders for their failures, forgetting that we get the kind of leaders we deserve. They think things would be better if we had different laws. Yet the law is what you and I make it, or what we let other people make it. Men who have lost faith in themselves try in vain to find something to blame for their failures.

A sick generation will believe in fate. They will insist that men are bound by chance, and are neither free nor responsible. But this kind of talk fools no one very long. To be sure, you can make a good case for the belief that man is helpless in the hands of fate. Once you grant the premise on which the fatalists base their case, you can argue for fatalism as well as for free will. The matter is not settled by argument, though, but by human experience, which is deeper than reasoning. Let any man come to the end of the day and look back over the day's events, and he knows that he made choices that day. He also knows that, to some extent at least, he was responsible for those choices. We cannot escape the certainty that God has made us free men, and that we must account for our lives.

This is precisely the human problem. We feel that we *must* do something we cannot do. As Paul puts it, we who feel we ought to be free men—indeed, must be free—are slaves to wickedness. We owe a debt to one who has a right to demand payment of us, but we cannot pay that lawful debt.

I am a child of God

Finally, through Jesus Christ, our eyes are opened, and we see the crowning truth about our lives—we are the children of God. We learn at last what we are, and the answer to the riddles of our nature. Made in God's image and created to have fellowship with him, through prayer we enter into our sonship.

32

Now we know we cannot stand alone because God has made us for himself. He has made us so that without him we are weak and not adequate for life. Perhaps some scientists who study the moon and stars can search the heavens and not see God. But no man can truly search his own heart without finding the evidence for God. When we say yes to him, we discover that

he giveth power to the faint; and to him that hath no might he increaseth strength. Even the youths shall faint and be weary, and the young shall utterly fall: but they that wait for Jehovah shall renew their strength; they shall mount up with wings as eagles; they shall run, and not be weary; they shall walk, and not faint. (Isa. 40:29-31.)

Henry George made a study of how great numbers of men grow poorer as a few men grow richer. In his book *Progress and Poverty* he says man is the only animal whose desires increase as they are fed. We are never fully satisfied here on earth, no matter how much we have. Forever we are under the spell of a divine discontent. Something within us soars beyond the earth; we long for a heavenly land. In short, our lives seem to be what we should expect them to be if we are children of God.

When we keep this central fact clear in our mind, all goes well. But when we forget it or neglect it, everything goes wrong. We can have a decent society in which men live as brothers only when men recognize that they are sons of God. Men fight for their freedom and keep the dictator down if they know they are God's sons and worthy of freedom. Democracy is possible only when it stands on a religious belief in the dignity and eternal worth of each man, because he is one for whom Christ died.

The young French social thinker Comte de Saint-Simon ordered his valet to wake him in the morning with these words: "Get up, monsieur le comte. Remember, you have great things to do."

So God in Christ says to every man, "Get up, and do the things that are worthy of a creature who is a son of Almighty God!" And when a man obeys this command, behold, his strength is as the strength of ten. He is able to fulfill the high and awful claims which his Lord and his own best self put upon him.

CHAPTER FOUR

I BELIEVE IN LIFE

OF ALL THE ARTS TO WHICH MEN GIVE THEIR TIME AND their talents the most neglected is the art of living. It is strange that men should care so little about something so important to them. Men with skilled training often prove to be the least fit to master the art of living. Tangled lives and damaged souls fill the offices of doctors and overflow our hospitals.

Yet the failures of these people are not failures of the mind. The men who fail to face life successfully are not always men of low intelligence. Some of the most brilliant people I know seem to have the least to live for. Some of the most gifted people end up in a dead-end street. The problem of meeting life successfully cannot be solved in the test tube. There is no easy, quick, and painless answer. Real living takes time. It is an eternal project, and we cannot put it off till some more convenient time. When it comes to learning how to live, we have no time to waste.

We must find the truth about life

Often we try to solve the problems of life simply by pretending they are not there. We try to get rid of them by shutting our eyes to them. This makes us feel released and happy for a short time. Why worry? But we cannot treat life this way for long. The playboy ends up in a bad way. Life is serious, and life is tragic. It will not hold back its anger forever, and the trifler finds, when it is too late, that he has been playing a game where the stakes are life and death.

The man who looks on the dark side of life misses the way just as surely as the silly optimist does. He sees everything except the main thing about life. Someone was showing a Chinese official the latest thing in X-ray equipment. "You can see all the bones in the body," he was told.

"Ah," the Chinese answered, "you can see all the bones, but you cannot see the heart."

The cynic sees all the parts, but he has a blind spot when it comes to seeing the meaning of the whole. We need help in looking at life. We need someone who can help us get a clear view. Otherwise we look through our faulty human eyes, and we see twisted images.

David Hume said: "Among a thousand different opinions that men may have on the same subject, there is but one just and true, and the only difficulty is to ascertain and fix it." Quite so! But it is very hard to find it. Yet, as far as life is concerned, the problem is solved in Christ. Jesus is the truth about life. When we need help, we can turn to him; when we are confused, he will guide us.

Jesus Christ was not the only one to say true things about life. But he combined wisdom and action as no other person ever did. We look at him and say, "This is life at its best. This is the way life ought to be." And looking unto Jesus, we find inspiration and the power to make our own lives great. At the time of the Trojan War, says Herbert H. Farmer, there were other women with eyes as beautiful as Helen's, and some with hair or complexion as beautiful as hers. But there was only one Helen, who combined beauty of eyes, hair, complexion, and form into one breath-taking loveliness that "launched a thousand ships." So is there only one Jesus Christ. He can inspire our lives, when they are bound in shallows and in misery, to launch forth on the ocean of God. He came that we might have life.

There is justice in life

Many people believe there is no justice in life, and they can defend their belief quite well. They will insist they deserve far greater rewards than they have received. Here is a man who certainly is not as good as they are, and he has prospered while they have not. Or they can list all the troubles that have come to them, and their neighbor has had no such trials. Why? They come to resent success of any kind and think it came through cheating or shady dealing. This is an easy attitude to take.

Bad luck does seem to dog the steps of some men. The burdens of life are not always distributed evenly. Some people carry a bigger load of tragedy than they ought to carry, and some seem strangely free from their share. Yet on the whole life is just, and we reap what we sow. Many a man who seems to deserve our pity does not want it and does not pity himself. And many a man who seems to have all the good things of life has an emptiness inside him, and no one envies him who knows him well. In the realm

37

of the spirit God tempers the wind to the shorn lamb. He gives us strength to bear our trials.

Usually we make our own trouble. I am not saying that we who suffer always mean to be bad men. But too often we have not learned what we do that is wrong. We have not been able to see what it is about us that causes trouble. We go from crisis to crisis, making the same mistakes and reaping the same sad results. We are often too lazy to ask what we are doing that so irritates others. Many of us would be saved from bitterness and defeat if only once we would assume that we were to blame. Then we could make an honest attempt to find out why and do something about it.

Of one thing I am certain: Self-pity is of the devil. The man who has learned to give in to this evil habit must rid himself of it before even God can help him. When we feel sorry for ourselves, we sign our own death warrant. Whether our day is bright or dark, whether our burden is heavy or light, we must face life with courage and gallantry. The poet Robert Browning believed defeat could be turned to moral victory. "For sudden the worst," he said, "turns the best to the brave." God has special rewards for those of us with heavy burdens, and he gives a special joy to sincere and humble men. Living with God makes any man rise above the discouragements of life.

Life tests us

In our time certain blithe spirits tell us that each man has a right to be happy, and should let nothing stand in the way of his happiness. The goal of all life, they insist, is happiness. Under the spell of such ideas men desert their families, deny their obligations, and drift lightly from one relationship to another. This selfish pursuit of happiness has led to the nonsense about setting up a new system of morals. This usually means that you do only what you want to do and refuse any unpleasant duty.

This does not work well, however, either for the people themselves or for their society. It seems you cannot get out of life what is worth having if you act like this, and no society made up of such people can last. The world is not made to support men who make happiness their final goal. We must be tougher men than this. We must be willing to accept our duties and our obligations to others. Our world is not friendly to weaklings who think only of themselves. When men are willing to desert their posts of duty for selfish profit, their civilization is headed for ruin.

Life is a testing ground, and God seems set on producing heroes. The blows we are called on to bear would not fall on us if God would rather have us happy than heroic. A wise man wrote long ago:

> My son, despise not the chastening of Jehovah;
> Neither be weary of his reproof:
> For whom Jehovah loveth he reproveth;
> Even as a father the son in whom he delighteth.
> —Prov. 3:11-12

Let us not envy the man whose life seems easy. Let us rather admire the man whose trials have made him strong.

Let us pray for an extra portion of strength from God. Our greatness of character is hammered out under the blows of ill fortune. Writers often do their best work in the face of irritations. Henry James did his best work when he dealt with Americans who irritated him. England, as Van Wyck Brooks said, was too pleasant for him. Life without struggle and difficulty would be unbearable. I agree with George Bernard Shaw, that an eternal vacation is a good working definition of hell.

The center of the Christian faith is a cross. On it a man died in agony and defeat. But in some strange way of God the cross has become the center of hope and comfort. That cross of Christ tells us that God meant for us all to carry our crosses—not because he hates us, but because he loves us and is testing us and training us for our eternal destiny.

We must run risks

If life is a testing ground, then it must be a place of risk. The possibility of tragedy and accident must be ever before us. Not everything that happens to a man is according to God's will. There are things which are even more tragic to him than they are to us. Suffering is the price God is willing to pay, and the price he has decreed we must pay, so that men may grow into freedom and character may be created. Freedom for us to err and to turn against him is the dangerous gift God has given us. It is the terrible risk he has taken, that our spirits may grow and commune with him.

So the world is not and cannot be a safe place to live. When we search for our security in the outer world, we search for what never can be found. Security is a thing of the spirit; it is born within us. Finally, our only security is in God. In vain do we try to make ourselves safe by gathering money or walling ourselves off from our fellows. We are all in this together. The innocent must bear the suffering of the guilty, and each man must bear the sins of all men. What good does it do us to curse our fate and cry out against life for being unfair? We must learn to see what God is trying to do, and we must accept our life on his terms.

Mahatma Gandhi was one of the saints of our time. This great leader, someone said, began each of his days with the following resolution:

I shall fear no one on earth.
I shall fear only God.
I shall hold ill will against no one.
I shall not submit to injustice, from wherever it may come.
I shall triumph over error by truth.
In resisting evil I shall never shun suffering.

When a man can start each day with these resolutions and do his best to live by them, he is learning the truth about life.

We must live the good life today

I believe in the greatness of life for this very day. I believe I can be as happy today as I can in the future. I

41

believe good chances for service and joy surround me *now*. I believe, if I will pray for it, that Jesus Christ will say to me as he said to Zacchaeus: "To-day is salvation come to this house" (Luke 19:9). I cannot know what a day may bring forth, but I do know that the time to do my duty and follow my Lord is *now*. Therefore let me proclaim my faith in life by doing the best thing which lies nearest at hand.

The Christian's belief in life tells him not to put off living. Filled with a sense of how great the gift of life is, he wants to make every minute count. It is a strange kind of paradox that because Christ gives us forever he makes each passing moment of lasting value. There is no better example of this than John Wesley. Samuel Johnson enjoyed stretching his legs and "having his talk out." And one day he got angry when Wesley walked away to pay a visit. But Wesley had a sense of what was at stake; he knew the seriousness of wasting one hour.

We do not live in an easy time. But people have had times of crisis before this one. As we look back on them, we can see that new life was coming to birth. No doubt those who were caught in those past periods of turmoil felt they were complete disasters. Yet in every such crisis there are people who face the tumult with a quiet faithfulness to their duties and an unshaken belief in God's rule over life.

Speaking of the Pilgrims' decision to leave Holland and sail for a strange, bleak land, William Bradford, their governor, said: "All great and honorable actions are ac-

companied with great difficulties, and must be both enter-
prised and overcome with answerable courages." I believe
that no matter what difficulties life puts in my way this
day, God will grant my prayer to make my courage
"answerable."

CHAPTER FIVE

I BELIEVE IN TOMORROW

MEN, WHEN THEY ARE SOUND, NEVER DOUBT THAT THEY are going somewhere. We are pilgrims without a permanent resting place here on earth. Men are not made to be content with the way they are or the way things are. When they are willing to settle down and adjust to present conditions, they have a kind of sickness. Religious men are always on the march.

A certain deacon always testified in prayer meeting: "I'm not making any progress, but I'm established." One day the deacon's buggy went into a mudhole, and he sat there, not able to move. One of his fellow church members came by and said: "Well, deacon, as you always say, you are not making any progress. But you certainly are established!"

G. K. Chesterton expressed the real truth about us when he wrote:

> For men are homesick in their homes
>   And strangers under the sun.
> And they lay their heads in a foreign land
>   Whenever the day is done.[1]

[1] Reprinted by permission of Miss D. E. Collins, Burns Oates & Washbourne, and Dodd, Mead & Company from *The Collected Poems of G. K. Chesterton*. Copyright, 1932, by Dodd, Mead & Company, Inc.

Jesus began his parable of the talents with the words: "For the kingdom of heaven is as a man travelling . . ." (Matt. 25:14 K.J.V.). There is a sense in which that broken sentence expresses a complete truth. We cannot long stay content with a way of life that does not change. When we come to a dead end, that is cause for despair. We cannot long endure without faith in tomorrow, and we cannot keep our spirits alive unless we can look to the future with hope. I believe that men cannot live without faith in a final plan and purpose in life.

Belief in tomorrow, of course, always involves risk. Tomorrow is something we cannot prove or define. We are tempted to live safely—which is to say, to live by the risks of others. We become mere dead weights on the backs of the pioneers. A man passing a group of loafers stumbled and nearly fell. They laughed at his clumsiness, and he joined in their laughter. Then he said, "I was nearly a goner, but I'm *going* somewhere. You fellows won't stumble—because nobody ever stumbled sitting down!" It is better to stumble and travel than to be safe and not go anywhere.

We are homesick for a future

A critic in the *Saturday Review of Literature* called his book review "Homesick for a Future." That title describes the mood of our time. It is a strange thing that in the day of our great prosperity, we are so fearful of tomorrow. That fear mocks our present comfort. Our mood is all the more bitter because our lack of certainty comes from what we thought was our chief virtue—namely, scientific cleverness. It shocks you through and through when the thing that was going to save you threatens your life—when your god bids fair to destroy you.

We are wise enough to know we cannot go back to more secure days. We cannot destroy what we have done; neither can we forget what we know. It is not practical to call a halt to military planning. We cannot go back to the war period and make our political decisions different. For better or for worse we have to begin where we are, with what we have, and keep our eyes forward.

Yet we cannot go on in the path we are following. Power is a two-edged sword that cuts the man who wields it as well as his victim. Our great power is clearly out of control. We have gained our goal; we have grown strong and successful. But we have not found the rewards we were promised. Instead our burdens grow heavier, and we grow less and less secure. Tomorrow is a nightmare.

We do not ask for a future without struggle. We know that life is not easy. We know that all gains of civilized man cost great effort and sacrifice. We are not looking for a dead equality or a world without danger. But we want our sacrifices to mean something, and we want the struggle to be more than civil strife. We want to believe we are leaving to our children something more than a third world war.

We must face the hard truth that the trouble lies with us. It is not the so-called heathen nations who have caused all the trouble. The disaster has come from the evil within Christian lands. We are the prodigal sons, and we remember our Father's house but dimly. We must find our way back to that house, which lies ahead on the road to the future for which we long.

We must travel new roads

One of the ancient poems of Israel says:

In the days of Shamgar the son of Anath,
In the days of Jael, the highways were unoccupied,
And the travellers walked through byways.
—Judg. 5:6

That was not the first nor the last time that men, for one reason or another, have allowed the straight ways to get lost in neglect. In our own time the highways to the full life are overgrown, and we vainly follow the bypaths. The human adventure is the building of roads to the good life. If we make any progress, it is as we discover the will of our God and then build ways that lead men to do his will. When we disregard his way, we too walk through byways.

There is nothing automatic about progress. We do not *have* to have a future. Life does not improve for men until they decide there are things which they will no longer endure. An easygoing taking of things as they are does not give us better men and women or a better society. At the root of all our effort we must have a vision of what men are and what they ought to be. The men who make sacrifices to gain the better life are men who decide there are some things they will not put up with any longer.

We need pioneers of the spirit—men like Isaiah, who had the faith and the vision to see and describe the new

47

road. He says: "And a highway shall be there, and a way, and it shall be called the way of holiness; the unclean shall not pass over it; but it shall be for the redeemed: the wayfaring men, yea fools, shall not err therein." (35:8.) We must follow that road, for it is the only way to the future we desire. It is the road to peace and security. It is the road to glory.

We live in God's world

Christians believe we owe both our money and our effort to God's kingdom. This doctrine appeals to our conscience and to our common sense. We must recognize that this world belongs to God and must be run in his name and according to his spirit. If we forget this, we destroy the earth and bequeath to the future poverty and famine. We cannot carelessly mine the land and destroy the timber without reaping dust bowls and floods. We may go through our natural riches like a swarm of locusts, but the next generation will hate us. The earth is ours to enjoy and to use, but if in our greed we waste its great riches, we shall bring punishment down on us all.

God is not a landlord who stays away, ignorant of what we are doing with his earth. He rules the ways of our life, and the world is under his control. When we respect the world he created, it becomes for us a garden. When we waste its riches selfishly or carelessly, it becomes a desert and a tomb. If the good earth is ever to become the home of a happy family, we must realize we are its stewards and not its owners. We must use it for God's purposes and not for merely our own.

48

If it limits us to realize the world is God's, it also frees us from worry about tomorrow. The world is our Father's, and it is never out of his control.

James Russell Lowell said: "I take great comfort in God. I think he is considerably amused with us sometimes, but that he likes us, on the whole, and would not let us get at the match box so carelessly as he does unless he knew that the frame of his universe was fireproof." Someone may say this was the case before the day of atomic bombs and iron curtains. But nothing has altered the fundamental fact of God's creation and control of his world. I believe that he can deal with atomic energy and with tyrants who deny him.

There is nothing in my life or yours that can make us certain of the future. We know no political wisdom or national humility great enough to support our hope for a better tomorrow. But, like Paul, we put our faith in God, who has laid his hand upon us in Christ. Then we can say with the apostle: "For I am persuaded, that neither death, nor life, nor angels, nor principalities, nor things present, nor things to come, nor powers, nor height, nor depth, nor any other creature, shall be able to separate us from the love of God, which is in Christ Jesus our Lord." (Rom. 8:38-39.)

We are going somewhere

What does all this we have been saying mean? It means that life has purpose. Life is not a moving in meaningless circles. There is a "far-off divine event" toward which we are moving. I do not always agree with my

49

Christian brethren who put so much stress on the second coming of Christ, especially when they become too definite about dates. But their stand reflects the Christian belief that life means something and the future holds promise.

All this points to the fact that goodness will win out in the end, and the sacrifices of the present are not in vain. It means, in the words of Micah, that "in the latter days it shall come to pass, that the mountain of Jehovah's house shall be established on the top of the mountains, and it shall be exalted above the hills; and peoples shall flow unto it" (4:1) .

Not everyone believes this is true. A Princeton philosopher wrote recently that he had come to the conclusion there is no purpose in life. He hinted that most modern men have decided about the same thing. However that may be, the sorry state into which life sinks when men can see no meaning in their lives proves that life cannot reach its best without faith in the future. And surely every true Christian lives in the light of an experience which proves to him beyond a doubt that God has a plan for each man. This experience is a gift from God to each of us who is humble enough to receive it. And if we once grasp God's plan for our own life, we cannot doubt the future he plans for all men.

God's great purpose runs through all of life if a man has eyes to see. William Cullen Bryant saw it in the flight of a bird:

He who, from zone to zone,
Guides through the boundless sky thy certain flight,

In the long way that I must tread alone,
Will lead my steps aright.

Jesus spoke of the care God takes even of birds, and then asked, "Are not ye of much more value than they?" (Matt. 6:26).

We make a great mistake when we try to "prove" that life has a purpose. The meaning of life is too big and too important to yield itself to our little mental exercises. Let a man follow Christ and he will never doubt that he is going somewhere that means something. The belief comes after the experience. There is a kind of life that cannot believe in the future because it is lived on too low a plane to see any purpose. Pride can blind our eyes to the eternal plan. But if like John Henry Newman we have made a spiritual quest out of our years, then we too can say:

So long Thy power hath blest me, sure it still
Will lead me on,
O'er moor and fen, o'er crag and torrent, till
The night is gone,
And with the morn those angel faces smile;
Which I have loved long since, and lost awhile.

Cicero said, "I care more for that long age which I shall never see than for my own small share of time." If this means we ought to neglect the present for the future, it is wrong. But if it means, as I think it does, that we need to aim beyond today in order to make today great, then Cicero was saying that faith in the future can light up the present for us. We need to feel the sense of the eternal in today's event to save it from the commonplace.

When Marshal Ney, favorite of Napoleon, was snubbed by members of the French nobility, he said with quiet assurance, "You are only descendants—I am an ancestor." It is a satisfying thing to be aware of our heritage. It means even more when we live with the belief in a great tomorrow. I believe with Paul that God "is able to guard that which I have committed unto him against that day."

CHAPTER SIX

I BELIEVE
IN IMMORTALITY

IT IS STRANGE AND WONDERFUL THAT THE THINGS A MAN believes in most are the very things he cannot prove or even express clearly. It is almost a rule that if you can explain a thing exactly, it does not mean much to you. The vital things are too real to be described. Because we cannot escape them, we have no power to make them plain to another person. That is why the important things of life are always private. We can feel them, but we cannot prove them. We can share them only with men whose spirits are in harmony with ours. I believe in immortality —in life after death. But I can only touch the edges of that faith when I talk about it.

What about my death?

There was a time when I thought it did not make any difference whether a person believed in immortality or not. I thought he could find a satisfactory way of life without thinking about the question of death. I did not see how it could make any real difference here and now. All this I repent of as one of the most shallow and stupid mistakes I ever made. The question of immortality is one of those final questions that face each man, and the answer he makes to it is laden with tremendous meaning for his life. No person who lives seriously can escape saying yes or no to the age-old question "If a man die, shall he live again?" (Job 14:14).

In one of his books Arthur Koestler tells about a meeting of Communist writers who were making speeches about the brave new world they were going to build according to Marx. Finally André Malraux broke in impatiently and asked, "What about the man who is run over by a tramcar?" His question was greeted by an embarrassing silence.

But there is a voice within us that we cannot ignore: "What about my death? What about the ones I've loved and lost?" To say that we can turn a deaf ear to such questions is to speak like a fool. A man has to believe *something* about what is going to happen to him when he dies. What he believes affects his every action and his every thought.

Jesus rose from the dead

The men who wrote the New Testament made much of the fact that Jesus rose from the dead. According to some modern critics they made too much of it. "Why," they ask, "didn't the Gospel writers tell us more about Jesus' life? Why did they talk so much about his last days, his crucifixion, and his escape from the tomb?"

The answer is that the early Christians knew it was the resurrection of their Lord that gave his life its meaning. We should not worry too much because they could not be exact and precise in telling what happened. Their ac-

54

counts are more believable because they carry the marks of men in the grip of a mighty spiritual experience—so sublime that words fail them and details are lost. But we cannot escape one fact: these men are writing about an event which convinced them absolutely that death had been conquered—which told them that because Christ lived, they too would live.

This is also the experience of modern Christians. Just as the risen Christ appeared to Paul "last of all, as to the child untimely born" (I Cor. 15:7), so he has appeared to Christians through the years. We too know him, though not in the flesh. But of course this experience cannot convince the man who has not had it. And we cannot package it and pass it on, or put it into a capsule to be swallowed. If a man would know, he must join the fellowship of Christ and accept him as king.

God has set eternity in our hearts

When we come to understand Jesus' life, we realize there is no hard-and-fast line between "living" and "dying." Jesus was always trying to make people understand that truth. Anne Morrow Lindbergh puts it like this in *The Steep Ascent:*

People "died" all the time in their lives. Parts of them died when they made the wrong kinds of decisions—decisions against life. Sometimes they died bit by bit until finally they were just living corpses walking around. If you were perceptive you could see it in their eyes; the fire had gone out. Yes, there were a lot of people walking around who were "dead" and a lot of people killed who were "living."

55

The pure in heart see God. The lowly in spirit are certain of his presence. The loved ones of Christ walk with him in an eternal experience *now*. The Christian knows all this, and no argument can convince him it is not true. The Christian feels in his heart that he was made for eternity, and his longings and hopes will not be satisfied with the partial satisfactions of this world. Certainly God has set eternity in our hearts, and unless every other experience with him is false, he will not suddenly shut the door upon us. Because we have learned to know he is willing to meet our deepest needs, we cannot believe that our glimpses of a better life are false. We are, as James Martineau said, overprovided for if this life is the end. The spiritual equipment of a man proclaims that he is made for an everlasting life.

Strangely enough, this belief grows stronger when we lose someone we love. I was never so sure of immortality as after my mother died. Who can describe such an experience as that! But let me say that her presence has been a constant reality to me ever since she left us. I myself have never had convincing proof that we can communicate with the dead. I am not saying I deny that we can—I just do not know. But I do not have the slightest doubt that the saints I have known are living still, and I shall one day see them again. As a great Christian, Peter Taylor Forsyth, wrote:

There are those who quietly say, as their faith follows their love into the unseen, "I know that land. Some of my people live there. Some have gone abroad there on secret foreign service, which does not admit of communications. But I meet from time to time the Commanding Officer. And when I mention them to him he assures me all is well."

No man can deny that the life after death is wrapped in mystery. A small child cannot possibly understand the joys of the adult. Neither can we grasp what life would be like without the stain of sin. Some of the great mystics have had visions which seem to tell us that when at last we see God as he is, we shall be transformed into his likeness. Paul said that we who are corruptible—we who are subject to decay and death—shall be made incorruptible. Beyond that we need not try to go.

We walk with a different step

A practical age like ours, which believes the final test of an idea is whether it works or not, ought to be convinced of the truth of immortality by the difference it makes in men's lives. The men who give something to the world, the men who are equal to life, always live as if they believe they will live forever. They are not too much concerned with what others call defeat. They seem to assume there are many things worse than death. This faith—often unspoken—makes them proof against hostile conditions or hostile men.

For one thing, when a man believes in immortality, he knows a peace the world cannot take away. People who have only today must get their profit now for fear they will not get it at all. This makes them irritable and worried. They search for some opiate to bring them peace of mind. But they never find it. What terrible things happen to the man who knows how short life is, yet has no faith in the future life! He is the man who falls under the sway of the jungle law. He cares about nothing but saving his own skin.

A housemaid had just been confirmed, and a friend asked her how she knew she was a Christian. "Because now I do not sweep the dirt under the rugs," she replied.

Perhaps someone might ask us how we know we are immortal. We might reply that when we take it for granted there will be another life, then life here makes sense, and we walk the earth with a different step. It works! Because almost every man feels this, men are driven to the wonderful belief that they will not die—even when it would be a great relief to believe, for the moment at least, that they will simply fall into a dreamless sleep.

This faith lights up all our life and gives a purpose to all our striving. O. Henry's last words were: "Turn up the lights; I don't want to go home in the dark." The faith that man can conquer death fills our life with a great light —a light that shatters the darkness of the fear of death.

Francis L. Patton, of Princeton Seminary, once pointed out that the high point of Old Testament faith in immortality lies in this verse from the twenty-third psalm:

Yea, though I walk through the valley of the shadow of death, I will fear no evil: for thou art with me.

Here is a desire to stay, but a willingness to go. Then Dr. Patton quoted Paul: "But I am in a strait betwixt the two, having the desire to depart and be with Christ; for it is very far better: yet to abide in the flesh is more needful for your sake" (Phil. 1:23-24) . This, Dr. Patton said, is a higher point yet, and it is the climax of New Testament faith in life after death. For Paul is saying that he is willing to stay, but he wants to go. Notice how the stress has changed. When a man can approach death with no holding back, he has found the experience which makes him conqueror over life.

We gain the long look

The hardest decision we have to make is to decide what things come first. We bring so many tragedies on ourselves because we cannot decide what matters we must never give up or compromise. It is too easy in this life for us to give up some sacred value in the name of being tolerant, only to find, when it is too late, that we have lost the main thing. Without it all our life is cheap and without point. But when we learn we are eternal creatures, we find the secret of wise choices.

There is this passage in André Gide's *Journals:*

I know a man whom a single thought sufficed to plunge into deepest melancholy, the single thought that, in the near future, he would have to buy a new pair of shoes to replace those on his feet. This man's case should not be considered one of avarice; what he felt was a sort of distress at not being able to stand on anything lasting, definitive, absolute.

If we stand on the certainty of eternal life, things like buying a new pair of shoes fall into their proper place.

When men are living at their best, they speak the language of eternity.

There are so many things people do that we can hardly call evil, but that are cheapening just the same. The bad man who makes a career of evil is rare. But the futile man who has nothing of nobility or grandeur in his life is all too common. It is this pettiness—this use of great resources for small goals—that marks our civilization and mars our personal lives. We do not seem to know what becomes us. I believe that until men have eternity in their hearts, they do not know what is fitting for them or for their society. It is a sad but sure truth that when men deny their faith in the other world, nothing goes right with them in this world.

We have a power of the spirit

Immortality means that things of the spirit are the real and lasting things. Perhaps this is the final question for us to decide. If we are only flesh and blood, then we are animals, forever chained to the earth, with no higher destiny than to return to the dust. But if we are spirits, then "it hath not yet appeared what we shall be." If we are spirits, then our power is not in our bodies but in our souls.

The evidence convinces me completely. Men are spirits, and they have a spiritual force that finally defeats the big battalions and the secret police. God has given them an immortal spirit as a bulwark against every enemy of mankind. This protects them against all mass movements which threaten to make slaves of men. It is as if God decided the spiritual nature of man was the final assurance that his human experiment would not fail.

Men may deny their spiritual nature for a time. They may seek to drown their awareness of it in a flood of physical sensations. But the one thing they cannot escape for very long is the power of their spirits. This is the guarantee of our kinship to God. This makes heaven as home to our souls.

There is an entry in the minutes of the annual conference of Methodist ministers in the year 1791 which reads:

Question 9. *Who have died this year?*
Answer: Wyatt Andrews—who died full of faith and the Holy
        Ghost. As long as he could ride, he travelled, and
        while he had breath he praised God.

That is all I know about this man, but no person could want a finer epitaph. Let a man travel as long as he can ride. Let him praise God as long as he has breath. Then let him die full of faith and the Holy Spirit. Against a life like that no power can stand. Death must give way before it.

I believe in immortality because of what I have seen of life and what I have felt in my own heart. But, most of all, I believe in immortality because of Jesus Christ, who was dead and is alive forevermore.

CHAPTER SEVEN

I BELIEVE IN TRIUMPH

ONE OF OUR MOST COMMON ERRORS IS TO MISTAKE A passing excitement for a lasting victory. We also tell ourselves we are getting something out of the dullest and most deadly undertakings. We start optimistically on paths which lead us nowhere but to sadness and regret. In the name of being up to date and worldly wise we go astray along the glittering paths of age-old sins. We lose our way because we get mixed up in our ideas of what is exciting and what is victorious.

G. K. Chesterton once said something that ought to be written on the mind of every person—especially every young person. He said, *"Morality is the most dark and daring of conspiracies."* Perhaps you never thought of it that way. Maybe morality seems like a dreary boredom to you—like a series of barren denials. Perhaps virtue seems like always saying no to what you would like most to do. But think about morality as an exciting plot, and see if that is not what it really is.

Civilization is an exciting plot

Rousseau was not the first man to cry out against the staleness of civilization and to praise the fresh, exciting life of the savage. When people get tired of themselves and worried about the future, they long for "the good old days." All who urge us to return to the simple things of savage times suffer from that same homesickness, though they usually put it into special language. But when you study the life the savage lived, with its hunger, its filth, its cruelty, its crudeness, its burning up of energy just to exist, you can see that civilization is an exciting plot to give men a chance to live.

Democracy is a daring experiment

When the dictators began to shout what they would do, and how soft and old-fashioned democracy was, too many of us—who should have known better—believed them. We were too much impressed with fancy salutes, rows of medals, goose-stepping, boasting. When our eyes were cleared, we saw that their police states were simply a return to the cutthroat jungle life that man has been struggling to escape.

If there is an exciting thing in the world, it is democracy. No man can prove it will last, but we cannot doubt it is one of the most daring experiments ever tried. It dares to believe that men can govern themselves, and that they can form a society where each man, regardless of class or race, can have equal opportunity. If "the wave of the future" belongs to the dictators, then the future has decided to go backward.

Marriage is a daring adventure

We give our young people the idea that marriage is nothing but a continuous thrill, an eternal honeymoon.

We glamorize the adolescents of the entertainment world who trip lightly from marriage to marriage. We make heroes out of people with emotions so childish and spirits so immature they cannot be faithful to their partners in marriage or to their own children. And then we wonder why there are so many divorces! We wonder what is wrong with the American home!

We must help young people look at marriage as a great conspiracy against the emptiness of casual and cheap relationships. Marriage began when a man and a woman saw the great values and great joys that are possible only within a home. They wanted something that took courage to achieve. The idea of a Christian marriage is one of the most daring things in the world, and it appeals only to those who seek adventure. When you see what happens to the people who flit from partner to partner, you know that those who make their marriage a lifelong creation of love and loyalty have chosen the best.

Prohibition is a daring venture

We sneered at the effort to do away with liquor, and in the name of personal freedom we destroyed prohibition. But what is the whole truth about the story of alcohol? The truth is that men and women with the pioneer spirit came to see that drink was a great enemy of the race. They saw ruined homes and broken lives. They said, "Let us do something about it. Why should we let this monster destroy our people?" So they dared to believe that one day we might see people freed from the power of this evil. Of course some people wanted things to stay as they were. But you cannot hold back progress forever, and the last word has not yet been spoken. In the meantime let us know that when we take our stand on the side of temperance, we label ourselves as ones who are going forward.

Evil is cowardly

As we learn more about criminals, we discover how important a part environment plays. But as Albert Schweitzer once remarked, no one gets a great idea without carrying it too far. We often assume that environment is the whole cause of crime and that no one is actually to blame for what he does. Too many of our social workers seem to think the only difference between a good man and a bad man is that one happened to be born on the wrong side of the tracks. The gospel faces facts more realistically.

Christianity says men are free and they make choices. It does not deny that some men have advantages over others; indeed, the gospel has been chiefly responsible for our reform movements and our sense of responsibility for other men. Yet when men choose the evil way, they choose what seems to them the easiest and cheapest way. They shun the hard path of right living, not because it is old-fashioned, but because it is hard. Great numbers of people prefer to take the easiest path and completely forget the final payoff. Usually such people feel very sorry for themselves and insist they have had the tough breaks when tragedy finally catches up with them.

In heaven's name, let us stop glorifying criminals! Let us stop making heroes out of gangsters. Let us show the evil path for what it is—the road to a cheap, temporary thrill

65

and a long heartbreak. Let us not take seriously those people who follow this path and then whine that life has no meaning and all human experience ends in bleak defeat. Harry Emerson Fosdick said, "Happiness is not mostly pleasure; it is mostly victory." Those people who choose the easy road for the sake of pleasure have no right to complain when the meaning goes out of their lives.

Evil is a return to things outgrown

In the long run, nothing is quite so boring as sin. What is more ridiculous and pitiful than the aging man who has dedicated his life to the pleasures of the body, when his body is no longer able to respond? How terrible is old age when it comes to the sinner, and how beautiful it is to the saint! Evil stands still, or turns backward. But goodness grows with the sunrise ever on its face.

I never made an evil choice I did not regret. I never made a good choice that did not go on paying dividends through the years. I have never been sorry when I have made what seemed to be a sacrifice of pleasure for the sake of duty. I have always been sorry when I failed to make such a sacrifice.

While Lord Northington was prime minister of England, he suffered a severe attack of gout. For a time he could not walk, and he said, "If I had known these old legs would one day carry a prime minister of England, I would have taken better care of them." Like a refrain that phrase "if I had known" rings through the experience of us all. Well, the Christian does know, though he may not always live up to what he knows. He knows from his own life and from the lives of others that a triumphant life cannot be based on evil.

The day of march has come

The Christian faith did not come into the world like a quiet meditation. It came like a trumpet call. Men who heard it did not always agree with it, but they were startled by it, and often upset. Christians saw the world as a battlefield where each man must choose his side and enter the struggle. He must fight the battle with banners flying. For God had spoken in a new way in Christ, and the day of march had come.

When Jesus called his disciples, he did not call them for a retreat into the quiet hills. They were not to be holy men who spent their hours only in meditation and prayer. Jesus' word was, "If any man would come after me, let him deny himself, and take up his cross, and follow me" (Mark 8:34). Jesus called for action and for self-denial.

Those who answered his call found in Jesus one who gave them a sense of victory over the world. In fact, one person called the disciples men who "turned the world upside down." They did not whine about the emptiness of life. The fear that gripped the first century had no power over them. Paul spoke for them and for Christians of every age when he said: "Wherever I go, thank God, he makes my life a constant pageant of triumph in Christ, diffusing the perfume of his knowledge everywhere by me" (II Cor. 2:14 Moffatt). These are words from a man who was far from safe and secure, but who had discovered that men need a belief in victory more than they need safety. The dark times held no terror, and Paul could say with General Wingate of Burma: "Times of darkness, mist, and storm—these are our times for achievement."

I believe in victory of the spirit

One of our greatest mistakes is to think that victory comes from physical might rather than from the spirit. We seek for triumph among the outer things, and all the time it has to come from within. Life has meaning when we are a part of some great purpose of God. No one has so much sheer joy as the person who has become a part of Christ's crusade.

Clement of Alexandria said that Christ turns our sunsets into sunrise. So he does. And he turns our weakness into power.

As I look back over the years, I think of the battles men have fought and the number they seemed to lose. I have not always been on the winning side. As a matter of fact, it seems that most of the time I have been with the minority. Yet I had rather be proud of a defeat than ashamed of a victory. I would not give up those experiences, defeats and all, for anything. I think of the comrades of different faiths with whom I have worked. I believe that all I am worth to myself and to God is what I have stood for and what I have fought for. When Christ called me to his service, he did not promise to keep me always on the winning side. He did promise to save me from boredom, futility, and despair. He has kept that promise, saving me from the gray wasteland through which so many of my brethren walk.

In John Bunyan's *Pilgrim's Progress,* Christian protects Little-Faith from Hopeful's severe judgment. He says: "No man can tell what in that combat attends us, but he that hath been in the battle himself. . . . But, I trow, you will put some difference betwixt Little-faith and the King's champion [Great-Grace]. All the King's subjects are not his champions."

Not all of us can be like Paul, nor by the wildest stretch of our imagination can we convince ourselves we are the King's champions. But with our few talents and small powers we are given the grace to be a part of the King's enterprises. We are given the assurance that he will win in the end, and our little lives become a part of the exciting plot to change the kingdoms of the world into the kingdom of God.

I believe in the victory of the spirit.

CHAPTER EIGHT

I BELIEVE IN FELLOWSHIP

THE CHRISTIAN VIEW OF LIFE IS BASED ON THE BELIEF that persons are worth more than anything else. In the eyes of Christ each man's life—yours, mine, any man's—is of lasting value. All Jesus' commands about how a Christian should act among his fellows stem from this deep root. The importance of persons is the completely new doctrine by which Christianity upset all pagan ways of life, and it is the basis on which Christians judge any society.

This means that when we deal with a man, we are dealing with an absolute—something beyond which we cannot go. God is in every human relationship, and many a man who has trouble finding God in the starry heavens above will be able to discover him in his neighbor. This means in our everyday life that as long as our personal relationships are wrong, everything is wrong.

We are made to live together

Until a man can say sincerely that he is "in love and charity" with his neighbors, as the communion ritual puts it so beautifully, no prayer can bring him peace of spirit or calmness of soul. John Wesley said that the Bible knows nothing of a solitary religion.

Even men outside the Christian fold have discovered the

truth of this Christian insight. A. E. Housman said in a lecture about poetry: "The greatest truth ever uttered and the most profound moral discovery of all time were the words of Jesus: 'He that findeth his life shall lose it: and he that loseth his life for my sake shall find it.'" Life holds many pitfalls for the man who thinks he can neglect people or treat them like brutes. The world is not a friendly place for the man who does not care about his brothers.

I was driving along a mountain road one autumn and came upon a flock of sheep being taken to the lower pastures for the winter. I met them at a narrow place with a sheer drop of a thousand feet or more on one side and a mountain wall on the other. I was impressed by the way the sheep stood quietly crowded together while I eased my car through them. One false move or one moment's giving way to blind fear and those on the edge would have gone over. I remembered reading somewhere that sheep often seem to sense when they must not give way to panic but must trust each other. The world leads men and women into such situations constantly. We are made to live together, and one selfish, frightened man threatens the lives of all.

Among the papers left by the novelist F. Scott Fitzgerald there was a list of suggestions for future stories. One paper read: "A widely separated family inherits a house in which they have to live together." This is the story which is being written today. Just substitute God for the author and the world for the house: "A widely separated family"—Russians, Germans, Chinese, Americans, Jews, Arabs—now live in a world so small that all the quarreling takes place right in our own living room. What the Bible calls "fellowship" is more than a word or an ideal. It is now the minimum requirement for living together.

"Aunt Cresy" got up in the revival meeting to tell about her dream. She was in heaven, standing in a long line of people. God was giving a crown to each one, and each crown was studded with shining jewels. But when she got her crown, it was plain. "Why doesn't my crown have jewels in it?" Aunt Cresy asked.

"Each of those jewels stands for another person brought to me," God said to her. "You came yourself, but you didn't bring anybody with you."

Aunt Cresy ended the story of her dream by saying: "I want you all to know that all day long I have been talking to people about going with me."

We must take other people with us, for we are all in this together.

The greatest sin is pride

The New Testament is quite plain on the subject of sin. No person who reads it has any doubt as to what the worst sin is. It is pride—pride which puts a man above God and above his brothers in his own mind. Jesus is terrible in his anger against the pride of spirit which regards men as means to an end, which uses men for selfish purposes. The men and women of the street, the ordinary sinners, will find mercy aplenty. But the "good" man who has no sympathy for weaker folks will face all the anger of a righteous God.

Men need our sympathy

There is a tendency for educated people to look on themselves as privileged persons who ought to be spared the unpleasant duties of life. One of the chief reasons why we need Christian colleges and Christian education is to train our young people in the principle of Christ: "And to whomsoever much is given, of him shall much be required: and to whom they commit much, of him will they ask the more" (Luke 12:48).

We dare not forget the word of Paul: "Now we that are strong ought to bear the infirmities of the weak, and not to please ourselves" (Rom. 15:1). Strangely enough, this Christian command to consider others does not limit us. It does not make our burdens heavier; it make them lighter. I believe that only as I dedicate my strength to the weak, my mind to the ignorant, my health to the sick, and my love to the unlovely—only then shall I know the riches of the love of Christ for me.

We do not live until we live in fellowship with men. When we can say of any man, no matter how evil or mean he is, "There, but for the grace of God, go I," then we have made it possible for God to work his miracle of grace in our hearts. Walt Whitman, who did so much for wounded soldiers during the Civil War, said: "I do not ask the wounded person how he feels. I myself become the wounded person."

We are wrong, though, if we think men always respond to good will. They do not. They did not all respond to Jesus. Many a man timidly tries to do good to another, and when that other seems to resent it or ignore it, the man wants to quit trying. The thing to do is to keep at it. There will be enough wonderful experiences to make up for the unpleasant ones, if you just keep on. There is much practical wisdom in the Chinese proverb, "All people are your relatives; therefore expect trouble from them."

Jesus reveals our own hearts to us as he shows us how to give sympathy to our fellows, even when they make it hard for us. Men need the sympathetic word and the understanding friend, even as you and I do. It is being cut off from their fellows that defeats them. Christ has saved us from loneliness by making us a part of his fellowship. We in turn must be, as Martin Luther put it, like Christs to our neighbors. I believe we begin to be saved when we start to share the longings and the misery of other men, in the name of our Lord.

The Church is the fellowship of Christians

It is a mistake to assume that Jesus organized the Church. He did nothing of the kind, and you will search the New Testament in vain for anything resembling a divine form of organization. The early Christians gathered themselves together in various forms. They adopted what seemed to work in the local situation. There never was the unity of organization that some people try to tell us marked the early Church. Jesus had little patience with men who thought form was more important than life. He would be just as impatient with modern Christians who think one denomination—one certain brand of religion—is more important than the fellowship of all churches that make up the one great Body of Christ.

But if Jesus did not organize the Church, he did something that means much more. He created it. That is, his spirit and teaching made it certain that his followers would join together in a fellowship. Jesus being what he was, and the gospel being what it is, the Church *had to be*—as certainly as a fig tree has to bear figs.

We do not all agree about the exact nature of the Church. We hold many different views. In his book *Prospecting for a United Church,* Bishop Angus Dun lists these three separate ways that people think of the Church:

First, the high-church or "catholic" point of view, which holds that God and man cannot find each other except through the Church.

Second, the Protestant idea, which sees the Church as the place where the true Word of God is preached and which believes the Word stands above the Church.

Third, the point of view which stresses the freedom of each believer and the final authority of his own inner experience, and regards the Church mainly as the fellowship of men whose hearts have been purified.

There are many different ways of looking at the Church. But however we look at it, we must never lose sight of the essential fact that the Church is a world-wide fellowship of men.

This fellowship is to strengthen us and comfort us. In Martin Luther's words, "Christ has not willed that the way of death, from which every man shrinks, should be solitary for us, but that we go the way of suffering and death with the whole Church as our comrade."

Yet we must not forget that the fellowship has another side to it. L. P. Jacks put it this way:

The Brotherhood of Man is not a crowd of friendly humanitarians. The Beloved Community is not a picnic. The Kingdom of God is not a mere collection of good people who believe in the Gospel of Jesus Christ. It is an exceeding great army of skillful, disciplined, highly competent men and women; not a standing army either, but a marching one, always on the move, always advancing with a united front, with perfect order as the keynote of the advance.

I take my stand with the Church

I believe in the Church. True, you can get terribly impatient with it and critical of its weaknesses. There are times when you can see it falter. It has its bitterness, its smallness, its narrowness, its hypocrisy. But when you look at other organizations, you come at last to see the church of Christ as our last, best hope. Just about all the worth-while things in our civilization had their beginning in the Church. And it is the Church that challenges the tyrant and champions the underdog. In the words of a great prayer for the Church: "When we compare her with all human institutions, we rejoice, for there is none like her. But when we judge her by the mind of her Master, we bow in contrition."

I believe in the Church. I believe that every man who knows he ought to do something about making the world a better place should be in the Church. I believe the

Church can add my own feeble efforts to the efforts of others and make them count for something.

Someone asked a deaf-and-dumb man, "Why do you come to church each Sunday when you cannot hear the service?"

He wrote out this reply: "I come each week to let people know which side I am on."

I want to be on the side of the Church. I need the comfort and inspiration of the Christian fellowship, and that fellowship deserves the best I can give it. Just as it is impossible to be an American without America, I believe it is impossible to be a Christian without the Church.

CHAPTER NINE

I BELIEVE IN LOVE

NOT THE LEAST SERIOUS EVIL THAT HAS BEFALLEN US IN this day is the murder of certain great words. Advertising, with its exaggerations, has made us shy away from some of the fine old words of our language. We are afraid they are being used simply to sell us something. The struggle going on in our time has affected our use of words. Truth is one thing to me but another thing to my enemies. Justice for my friends is not quite the same as justice for strangers. Right is what I do, but the same thing suddenly turns into wrong if my opponents do it. This murder of words puts walls around us, shuts us away from people. We cannot talk to other men unless they understand what we mean by the words we use.

What do we mean by "love"?

One of the words we should rescue and clean up is the word "love." Modern use has made it such a sloppy, sentimental word that the phrase "the love of God" has no meaning to many a modern person. The phrase "love your neighbor" makes us see a nosy reformer who wants to meddle in everybody else's life—especially the poor. Most of us respond to that sort of thing the same way the English workman did. He said, "I don't want to be done good at!"

The word "love" in the New Testament sense is a great and saving word. It means interest and sympathy and good will. It is not a word for weaklings but for strong men. It means a positive search for a chance to show good will to a person. It is the only foundation on which we can build a satisfactory life with other people; without it our efforts are in vain.

When we feel love, we find our vision cleared and we see things as they are. Until we love men, we cannot know them. Until we love God, we cannot see him. More significant than knowledge is love.

Christian love is something we are *commanded* to practice. Jesus does not say, "It would be nice to love," or "I wish you would try to love," or "If it is possible, you should love." He says: "Thou shalt love the Lord thy God with all thy heart, and with all thy soul, and with all thy mind. This is the great and first commandment. And a second like unto it is this, Thou shalt love thy neighbor as thyself." (Matt. 22:37-39.) That means love is something we must practice as a matter of obedience. It is something not confined to our personal feelings; it is to be done whether we feel like it or not. We have to learn how to love by making ourselves practice love.

We learn to love God and men at the feet of Jesus. If we try to love the unlovable by our own will power, we shall have a bad time of it. Love is a matter of the will, it is true, but it demands the gentle yet firm power of God to make it work.

A priest who ministered at an insane asylum often served Communion to the poor slobbering idiots. A friend said, "I don't see how you can stand this terrible place and these terrible creatures."

"I have learned to see their broken minds as God must look upon all of us who are incomplete and idiotic in our preference for evil," the priest answered.

Men saved by the love of God are able to look at men —any man, all men—through the eyes of Christian love.

Love is reverence for life

Recent history shows what horrible things men can do to their brothers when they lose their faith in God. We have been through a war in which a spiritually bankrupt people seemed determined to destroy themselves. The denial of human rights and the use of torture did not take place in Africa but in Europe. It was not the South Sea Islanders who declared war on civilization, but men with Christian backgrounds. Christian nations used war, destruction, death, to settle quarrels among themselves. And a Christian system which denies love denies its Lord. Such a system cannot endure.

Albert Schweitzer, certainly one of the great men of our time—and of all time—has gone against all our popular ideas of success. Schweitzer is a great organist and an authority on Bach, but he left the concert halls of Europe to serve the ignorant natives of Africa. He is a first-rate New Testament scholar and a world-famous thinker. But he studied to be a doctor, so he could heal the sickness of poor ignorant men who never could appreciate him—let alone pay him back.

There on the edge of the forest Albert Schweitzer

thought deeply about the real secret of life. Finally it came to him like a revelation, one day while he was on a river boat. He gave us that great phrase: *reverence for life.* All life, he insisted, is precious in the sight of God, and killing is a denial of God. This, it seems to me, is just another way of telling us that love should be the foundation of all man's actions. Men must have love if they are to come into the new Kingdom instead of wandering in a desert where nothing worth having could survive.

It is easy for us to see the striking difference between Schweitzer and Hitler, both of them products of our time. Hitler's spirit was to kill as many thousands of people as necessary in order to give his nation its place of power. We do not have to be very smart to see the difference between these two men. But, sad to say, in spite of our protests and our fine claims our hearts belong to Hitler. We speak of peace, but we want the things which produce war. We would like a warless world, but we follow the path leading the other way. We are not willing to make the big effort it takes to learn to love all men, and thus bring peace into our own hearts—where peace has to begin.

When men have no reverence for life, they can have none of the conditions for establishing freedom. With clear insight Judge Learned Hand said:

The spirit of liberty is the spirit which is not too sure that it is right. The spirit of liberty is the spirit whch seeks to understand the minds of other men and women. The spirit of liberty is the spirit which weighs their interests alongside its own without bias. The spirit of liberty remembers that not even a sparrow falls to earth unheeded. The spirit of liberty is the spirit of Him who, nearly 2,000 years ago, taught mankind that lesson it has never learned, but has never quite forgotten; that there may be a kingdom where the least shall be heard and considered side by side with the greatest.

This great jurist relates the spirit of liberty to the concern and love of Jesus. We shall not have the one without the other.

A French prime minister was about to have an operation. He said to the surgeon, "You will, of course, treat me more gently than you do the poor miserable wretches in the hospital."

The surgeon replied, "Sir, every one of those poor miserable wretches, as Your Eminence is pleased to call them, is a prime minister in my eyes."

Let us never forget that love for men and reverence for life is the principle of survival—to place it no higher. And let us remember, too, that love has to begin in our hearts and express itself in our dealings with each man we meet.

Love is the strongest force

When Jesus used the method of love, he did not choose it because it is "nice" or because he was overly tender. He chose it because it is the strongest and most enduring force in the world. He saw things as they are. George Herbert wrote, "Love rules his kingdom without a sword." Love seems to be so simple and so modest that many a tyrant has been fooled by it. Love blows no trumpets, and as Paul said:

Love suffereth long, and is kind; love envieth not; love vaunteth not itself, is not puffed up, doth not behave itself unseemly, seeketh not its own, is not provoked, taketh not account of evil. . . . But now abideth faith, hope, love, these three; and the greatest of these is love. (I Cor. 13:4-13.)

The universe is built on the principle of supporting those things that will endure. The sudden flash of power, the victory won in a moment, often end as quickly as they began. Success belongs to those who have staying power, and can wear down the strength of their enemies. It is this power to endure and patiently wait that makes love win out in the end.

More and more it seems to me that real living is chiefly a matter of having courage to hold on when you do not want to hold on. The brilliant man with no staying power is not a safe bet. No man has a more shaky future than the one who will not see a job through before running off to try something new. The foundation of the good life has to be something tough.

There are times when a man cannot stand things any longer, and a bitter rebellion rises in him like a tempest. What does he do then? He prays. The life of prayer is the life of power. Men who believe that praying is only a matter of last resort do not know how mighty prayer is when it becomes a habit. Men who have discovered how weak they are may know the satisfaction of having a sure protection against their weakness. They "take it to the

Lord in prayer." Men who live by the law of love live in constant close fellowship with God through prayer.

We must love our neighbor

We must be careful not to think Christian love is something vague and general. Christian love is specific and practical. It is not love of an "idea" or "principle." It is love of persons—not persons in general, but people one by one. Too many of us talk about loving humanity, but do not love the man next door. Young couples who turn their homes into bickering battlefields may show great concern about the United Nations. Yet how silly it is for them to talk about nations coming together when the two of them, who love each other, cannot live in unity and peace!

We should do what Jesus suggests in the parable of the good Samaritan. The Samaritan did not go home and make a survey, or refer the case to the organized charities, or write a letter to the paper. He upset his own plans, delayed his own journey, and spent his own money to put his love into action right then. Maybe you think an act like this is a little thing. But let me tell you that such an act is contagious and spreads with the speed of light. It is amazing how many of our great reforms began with some simple deed of love.

In our day of trouble let us realize we cannot make things right with bombs and forced military service. There are vast numbers of people in the world too ignorant to understand a set of ideas or too listless to care what different parties stand for. But they will certainly understand food for the hungry, clothes for the cold and ragged, medicine for the sick, books for the mentally starved.

I believe I have a duty to my world and a chance to play an important part in healing the sickness of men. I must begin by loving my neighbor.

Love gets results

Love is not something you have to force on a person against his true wishes. Every man wants love. It is in harmony with his true nature. When Jesus speaks of the hunger to love and be loved, he is describing me and every man. Love is what we really want.

Love is not cheap. Indeed it is one of the most costly things in the world. It costs much to give and it costs much to receive, because it puts a man forever in its debt. But since we measure cost by what we get, we know that what we spend for love is the best bargain we ever made. I know that love brings fulfillment and joy. I am never so intensely alive as when God's love is having its way with me. Bitterness and hatred cripple and kill the man who harbors them, but "we also rejoice in our tribulations: . . . because the love of God hath been shed abroad in our hearts" (Rom. 5:3-5).

CHAPTER TEN

I BELIEVE IN FAITH

FAITH IS ONE OF THE NECESSARY THINGS. THE BOOK OF Hebrews gives what is probably the best-known definition, and it tells us a great deal. Faith, it says, is an assurance and a conviction about things you cannot see. It makes you feel sure about things you cannot prove. It is not believing something you would merely like to believe, nor hoping that your "wishing will make it so." It is more like an open-eyed venture out beyond the limits of your knowledge. It is risking your life for values that mean more to you than safety.

What is faith?

Faith suggests loyalty to certain truths in spite of changing moods. None of us admires the unstable fellow who does only what he feels like doing. He is not a good worker and he is not a good friend. We love and trust the man who chooses a pattern of conduct and then sticks to it. This faithfulness is one of the foundation stones of the good life. A man cannot establish and maintain anything of lasting worth until he decides he will live by certain principles whether he feels like it or not.

Faith is belief, if we define our beliefs as the things we live by. Faith is not a mental exercise, or a vague senti-

ment, or a creed which has no noticeable effect on our
living. Faith is the system of values we have sworn alle-
giance to, the system of values we will not deny.

When Paul says we are saved by faith, he does not mean
we are saved by repeating certain statements about Jesus.
He means that we are saved because God did something
for us in Christ—something we could not do for ourselves.
He means that we are saved by a complete response to
Christ. One of our great Christian thinkers, Herbert H.
Farmer, puts it in these words: "Faith is that attitude of
mind which, finding itself laid hold of by the truth con-
cerning God's love as given through Christ, commits itself to that truth in adventurous trust and obedience, in
spite of all the mystery and all the perplexity that remain."

We live every day on faith

Men often make the mistake of thinking religion is
the only field where men have to resort to faith. They
are sure that "practical" things like science deal with
facts, but religion has to deal with what men cannot prove,
therefore with what is not practical. They do not go
quite so far as the boy who defined faith as "believing
something you know ain't so." But they draw a clear line
between knowing and believing.

Let me say at once that all of this is a terrible mistake.
Science rests on faith just as much as religion does. Every
great scientist acts on ideas he cannot prove. Who ever saw
a light-year? Who ever traveled to even the nearest star?
How do I know there is such a thing as an atom? In all

these cases we believe things we cannot see; we leap far ahead of the actual observable facts.

What is a law of science or a law of nature? It is taking for granted that, since we have seen a great number of cases in which A causes B, we can act on the belief that A will always cause B. But one day A causes something slightly different from B, and we have to change our law. We have discovered new data. Science goes as far as it can to prove things. Then, like everything else, it acts on the basis of an "assurance of things hoped for, a conviction of things not seen."

All of our everyday life is lived on faith. Business could not last five minutes without credit, and credit is another name for faith. If we always had to put the cash on the line, what would happen to our complicated business system? What would happen to banks and checking accounts? We do not live a single hour without acting on the basis of things we believe but cannot prove. Men cannot live together without trust, and we are learning today that nations cannot live together without faith.

How many of the gadgets of civilization would we use if we had to understand them first? I for one could not use the telephone, or look at television, or listen to the radio, or drive a car, or turn on an electric light, if I had to explain first how these things work. I do not know how they work, but I use them. When things go wrong and our machinery breaks down, we resent it and feel hurt, as if something has betrayed us. What we believed in has proved to be unworthy of our faith.

Someone may say to us, "Religion is based on faith."

We can reply, "Of course. And so is everything else." And, like everything else, religion is judged by its fruits. When I venture forth in the name of my religion to find out more about God, I follow the same general path the scientist or any sincere seeker of truth must follow.

We cannot live on doubt

A generation in love with the scientific spirit tries to avoid making choices. It prefers to commit itself to nothing. Why not doubt everything, it seems to ask, and proceed on the basis of trial conclusions? Why commit your life to any faith? Why act as if you believe anything? And all this sounds so smart, so worldly wise, so advanced, that we are impressed. We turn up our noses at the faith of our fathers, and we look down on all who venture into the unknown.

But the answer to this way of life is simple and final: it will not work. We cannot endure life lived without faith. If we try to live on a trial basis, our life limps. God created men to believe and to dare, and man's spirit loathes emptiness. We will believe *something* whether we mean to or not. The only choice we have is which faith we shall make our own.

Jesus has a word for us that we should never forget:

But the unclean spirit, when he is gone out of the man, passeth through waterless places, seeking rest, and finding it not. Then he saith, I will return into my house whence I came out; and when he is come, he findeth it empty, swept, and garnished. Then goeth he, and taketh with himself seven other spirits more evil than himself, and they enter in and dwell there: and the last state of that man becometh worse than the first. Even so shall it be also unto this evil generation. (Matt. 12:43-45.)

This is our Lord's warning as to what happens to empty men and empty generations.

More times than not our misery is the revenge our neglected talents are taking on us. We know vaguely that something is wrong, but we will not take positive steps toward a better life. We cannot have happiness without faith, and the frustrated men and women among us are the people who have never had a dream take hold of them.

We must make a choice

The English novelist Arnold Bennett says:

A man may desire to go to Mecca. His conscience tells him that he ought to go to Mecca. He fares forth either by the aid of Cook's or unassisted. He may never reach Mecca. He may drown before he gets to Port Said; he may perish ingloriously on the coast of the Red Sea; his desire may remain eternally frustrated. Unfulfilled aspirations may always trouble him. But he will not be tormented in the same way as the man who, desiring to reach Mecca, and harried by the desire to reach Mecca, never leaves Brixton. It is something to have left Brixton. Most of us have not left Brixton. We have not even taken a cab to Ludgate's Circus.[1]

[1] From *How to Live on Twenty-four Hours a Day.* Used by permission of the owner of the copyright, Hodder & Stoughton, Ltd., and Doubleday & Co., Inc.

Until we have committed ourselves—until we have left Brixton—we have not begun to live. We must choose the faith we will live by.

Which faith shall we choose?

I am not advising you to accept just any old thing and believe in it. Many people in our time have been so hard put for a faith that they have accepted the evil nonsense of Fascism and Communism. That should be warning enough to us. No good thing can come out of an evil belief. As G. A. Studdert Kennedy said, "It is much easier to do and die than it is to reason why." We need to use all the sense and judgment we have. We should take nothing for granted that we can test and try.

A scientist and his friend were traveling in Wyoming when they saw a flock of sheep on the mesa. "They've just been sheared," said the friend.

"They seem to be—on this side," was the cautious reply of the scientist.

Such a spirit is not contrary to the spirit of religion.

But let us stop talking such nonsense as "it does not matter what a man believes just as long as he is a good man!" Men are what they believe. When any person says, "I believe this," or "I believe that," the issues of eternity hang in the balance. Christians who claim that right thinking about God is not important are too simple-minded to be allowed loose. They are the people who are helpless in the face of rascals with crude but vital faith.

The only answer to an evil idea is a good idea. The only defense against the Communists is a democracy in which

91

people are really committed to the principles of freedom. Which is to say that only Americans can destroy America. Only Christians can destroy the Church. For when we do not believe in Christianity enough to live it, all sorts of devils and false gods—Communism, Fascism, secularism— will fill the emptiness.

In a world like ours, full of clashing faiths, no man can stand in a neutral corner. We must join one side or the other. Either we take a stand on the Christian side to fight for the dignity of man, or we choose the side of the enemies of man. For evil draws its greatest support from the men who do not really want evil but who are too lazy to fight it. Always, if we have eyes to see, there stands Christ on the one side and his enemies on the other, each trying to win our support. We make a choice, even when we think we will not choose either side.

The Christian faith will hold us up

I believe in the Christian faith. I believe it is the ultimate truth about God, man, and life. I believe that Jesus Christ is the truth. I believe that the history of the Christian faith proves that it comes from God. I believe that every event of the past two thousand years supports what the Christians have said. I believe that God in Christ saves men and saves the world. I believe the gospel is not one way among many, but *the Way* to the good life. I believe the gospel is the answer to the most profound questions man can ask, and it gives enough light for him to live by.

When the little optimistic creeds give way under the strain of terrible burdens, the Christian faith stands firm as always. It is not a faith just for sunshine and prosperity. It shines with more brightness when everything seems to go wrong. It begins with the worst and faces the blackest facts in man's experience. It is the most realistic and honest view of life I know. It is made for the hardest going. When things are at their worst, the Christian faith shines out against the dark, with all its grandeur and power.

A German pastor said when he got out of a concentration camp:

I cannot tell you how thankful I am for the inner experience I have been permitted to have in these days. . . . How good it is that our faith may now manifest itself really as faith —not merely in words, but in deeds and attitudes. . . . No one will be able to say any more what formerly in foolishness was sometimes said: "He merely talks that way because he is paid for it."

The faith that holds up in time of crisis is the faith for me.

The limitless riches of Christ come to me and to you through prayer. When we learn to draw from God's storehouse of power, that power begins to flow into our lives. A quiet time each day pays us tremendous dividends. Only a fool says he does not have time enough to pray. We can afford to leave many things undone, but not this. We can decide for ourselves when and where and how we can pray best. But we must learn to go to God and accept the new life he will give us. Prayer mends our broken lives and makes us able "to walk and not faint." It makes us sure that God is with us, and lets him be our friend and our strong defense.

An old man and his young helper were working on a roof. The man laid a ladder with spikes under it across the sloping shingles. Then he told the boy to step out on it. When the boy hesitated, the man said, "Step down on it, my lad. See how it holds. The heavier the load, the better it holds you up." So it is with the Christian faith. No matter how heavy our load, it will hold us up. Its power redeems our lives.